Fact Finders®

The Story of the
Civil War

GREAT WOMEN
of the CIVIL WAR

by Molly Kolpin

CAPSTONE PRESS
a capstone imprint

Fact Finders Books are published by Capstone Press,
1710 Roe Crest Drive, North Mankato, Minnesota 56003
www.capstonepub.com

Library of Congress Cataloging-in-Publication Data
Kolpin, Molly.
 Great women of the Civil War / by Molly Kolpin.
    pages cm.—(Fact finders. The story of the Civil War)
 Includes bibliographical references and index.
 Summary: "Describes key women involved in the American Civil War, including workers of the Underground
Railroad, spies, abolitionists, and battlefield nurses"—Provided by publisher.
  ISBN 978-1-4914-0719-6 (library binding)
  ISBN 978-1-4914-0726-4 (pbk.)
  ISBN 978-1-4914-0730-1 (ebook pdf)
 1. United States—History—Civil War, 1861-1865—Women—Juvenile literature. 2. United States—History—Civil
War, 1861-1865—Biography—Juvenile literature. I. Title.
 E628.K65 2015
 973.7082—dc23   2014007635

Developed and Produced by Focus Strategic Communications, Inc.
    Adrianna Edwards: project manager
    Ron Edwards, Jessica Pegis: editors
    Rob Scanlan: designer and compositor
    Karen Hunter: media researcher
    Francine Geraci: copyeditor and proofreader
    Wendy Scavuzzo: fact checker

Photo Credits
Corbis, 5, Lebrecht Music & Arts/Lebrecht Authors, 27; Deborah Crowle Illustrations, 7, 19; Getty Images Inc: Dennis
Macdonald, 12, MPI, 14; The Granger Collection, NYC, 24, 25; Library of Congress: Prints and Photographs Division,
11, 21, 23, 28; North Wind Picture Archives, 29; Public Domain, 9, 17; Shutterstock: Christophe Boisson, stars and
stripes design

TABLE OF CONTENTS

WOMEN ENTER THE WAR

Starting in 1861 the Civil War raged across the United States for four years. The country was torn in two. Northern states fought against Southern states. Neighbors fought neighbors. Brothers fought brothers.

Women also entered this war zone. Women on both sides of the battle lines played vital roles. Many took up active roles on the front lines. They provided care to soldiers. They spoke out against inequality. They risked their lives to free black people who were forced into slavery. They took on dangerous roles as spies.

So what made these women want to help the war effort? What was all the fighting about? And why was the United States a divided nation? Answers to these questions date back to 1860.

front line: the area nearest enemy fire

inequality: lack of the same rights for everyone

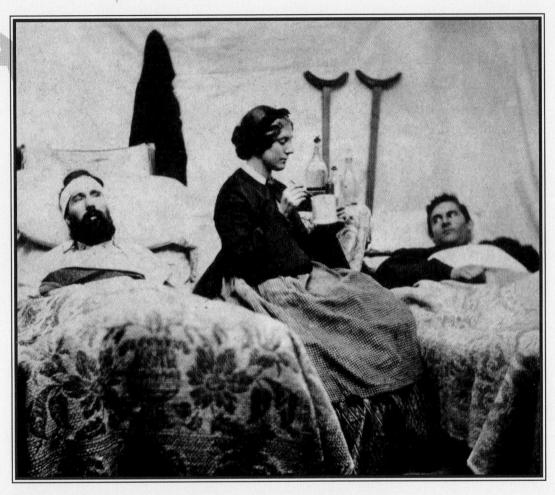

Women played many roles in the Civil War, including tending to wounded soldiers.

On the Brink of War

On December 20, 1860, South Carolina became the first Southern state to secede from the United States. Over the next six months, 10 more Southern states would follow. These were the Confederate States of America, also known as the Confederacy. The Northern states remained the United States of America, also called the Union.

The main issue dividing the North and South was slavery. By the mid-1800s most Northerners opposed slavery. Black people were brought to the United States from Africa against their will. They were bought and sold as slaves. They were often ill treated by their owners.

Southerners, however, needed slaves to help them work their farms. They knew their plantations would not succeed without help from slaves. But they feared the government was going to end slavery. This fear led them to secede. They wanted to form their own country and government. Northern states, however, wanted the nation to remain united. The issue became so heated that by April 1861, the United States was at war.

secede: to withdraw formally from a group or an organization, often to form another organization

plantation: a large farm found in warm areas; before the Civil War, plantations in the South used slave labor

6

THE UNITED STATES DURING THE CIVIL WAR

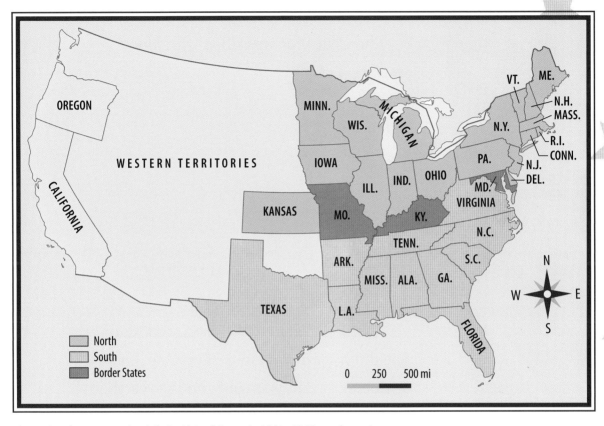

The 11 Southern states that left the United States in 1860–1861 are shown in gray.

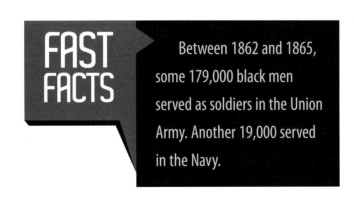

FAST FACTS

Between 1862 and 1865, some 179,000 black men served as soldiers in the Union Army. Another 19,000 served in the Navy.

CHAPTER 2

FIGHTING WORDS

The Civil War was filled with bloody warfare. But while men battled each other with weapons, women found other ways to fight. Some chose to enter the war through their words. They used their writing, speeches, and stories to sway public opinion. These women proved that the pen can really be mightier than the sword.

Harriet Beecher Stowe

Harriet Beecher Stowe was not a slave. She did not grow up in a slave state. She was a white, married woman from the Northern state of Connecticut. She was also a busy mother of seven children. Few people would have expected her to write a book about slavery that would change the United States. But that is exactly what she did.

Harriet Beecher Stowe

9

Stowe did not grow up around slaves. However, she knew about the issue of slavery. As a child she had heard her father preaching antislavery sermons. Stowe was a gifted writer with a vivid imagination. She knew she could use her talents to show how bad slavery was. In 1852 she published a book called *Uncle Tom's Cabin*.

Stowe's book told the story of a slave named Uncle Tom and his cruel master, Simon Legree. It showed readers how awful and unfair slavery was. Northern abolitionists praised the book. Southern slave owners condemned it. People began to debate slavery. Some people believe Stowe's book started the Civil War.

No one knows if Stowe actually set out to start a war. But she was determined to spread her antislavery message. She even wrote a column for a newspaper called *The Independent*. She used this column to speak out bravely against slavery.

abolitionist: a person who worked to end slavery

Uncle Tom's Cabin became a very popular book. More than 300,000 copies were sold in the first year. This was a huge number for its time. The book was read by people around the world.

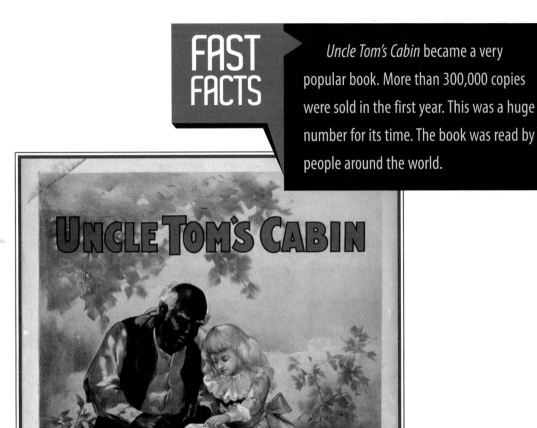

The book *Uncle Tom's Cabin* showed the world how unfair slavery was.

Sojourner Truth

Stowe wasn't the only woman to speak out before the Civil War. Sojourner Truth was another strong female voice in the antislavery movement. She was born into slavery in New York around 1797. In 1828 New York outlawed slavery. Truth became a free woman. She moved to New York City and worked as a housekeeper.

This powerful monument to Sojourner Truth is located in Battle Creek, Michigan.

FAST FACTS

Soon after gaining freedom, Truth learned that her young son, Peter, had been illegally sold to a man in Alabama. She took Peter's case to court and won. It was the first time a black woman successfully challenged a white man in a U.S. court.

Everything changed for Truth in 1843. That year she decided to preach about inequality. She claimed it was a mission given to her by God.

Soon Truth was speaking out against slavery. She was inspired by the speeches of famous abolitionists Frederick Douglass and William Lloyd Garrison. These men knew how to command a room—and so did Truth. She never let being a woman hold her back. She stood 6 feet (1.8 meters) tall. Her size and powerful voice captured the attention of audiences.

Truth didn't stop at speeches. She also told her life story to a writer. In 1850 her autobiography, *Narrative of Sojourner Truth*, was published.

autobiography: a book in which the author tells about his or her life

After the Civil War ended, Truth had a new mission. She wished to help the newly freed slaves. She also fought for women's suffrage. Her energy and leadership helped the United States become free and fair for everyone.

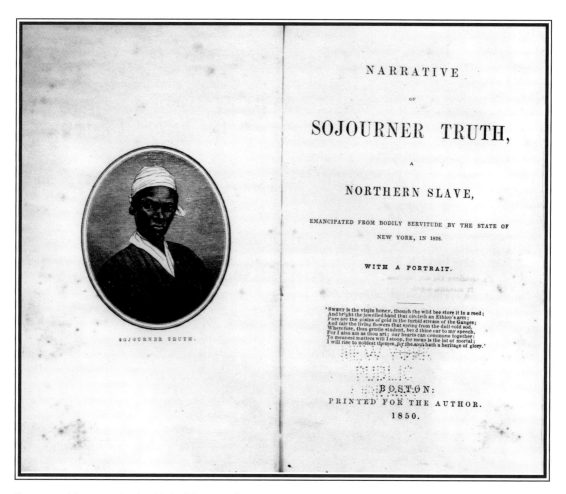

Narrative of Sojourner Truth told the life story of this amazing antislavery advocate.

suffrage: the right to vote

A Segregated City

During the Civil War, Truth traveled to Washington, D.C. She hoped to end the city's segregation of public transportation. She believed blacks and whites were equal. There was no reason they should not sit side by side.

It is said that Truth once stopped traffic when she wasn't allowed to board an all-white trolley car. She refused to move and convinced the crowd to support her. Her stubbornness paid off. Finally, Truth was allowed on board.

segregation: the practice of keeping groups of people apart, especially based on race

CHAPTER 3

FREEDOM GUIDE

Slavery ended in 1865 with the end of the Civil War. But one woman wouldn't wait for freedom to come. She decided to bring freedom to others. She risked her safety and helped hundreds of slaves find freedom. Her name was Harriet Tubman.

Harriet Tubman

Around 1820 Tubman was born into slavery in the state of Maryland. During her years as a slave, she was often punished harshly. She also saw other black people being mistreated. One day she'd had enough. When another slave was about to be beaten, Tubman spoke up. The supervisor was furious. He punished Tubman by breaking her skull. For days after the incident, Tubman was unconscious. She experienced blackouts for the rest of her life.

Harriet Tubman (far left) is shown in 1885 with her family and some of the slaves she was able to free.

By 1849 Tubman was desperate to be free. When she heard that her owner was going to sell his slaves, she decided to act. She planned to escape with her two brothers. In the dark of night, they ran away from the plantation. They relied on the light of the North Star to guide their path.

During the journey Tubman and her brothers lost their courage and turned back. Later Tubman escaped again, but this time alone. She knew that dogs were probably on her trail. She also knew she would receive her worst punishment yet if she was captured. But after a long and frightening trip, Tubman made it to Philadelphia. She was finally a free woman.

In Philadelphia Tubman worked as a housekeeper. But she had another important job too. During the 1850s Tubman secretly worked on the Underground Railroad. The Underground Railroad was a network of safe places where black people fleeing from slavery could rest.

FAST FACTS

Harriet Tubman was also a spy. As the Civil War raged on, she organized former slaves to watch Confederate troops. They gave information to Tubman. She then passed it along to Union military leaders.

It would have been easier for Tubman to stay safely in Philadelphia. Instead, she risked her life helping others find freedom. Tubman bravely returned to Southern slave states 19 times. She helped more than 300 black people escape slavery.

UNDERGROUND RAILROAD ROUTES

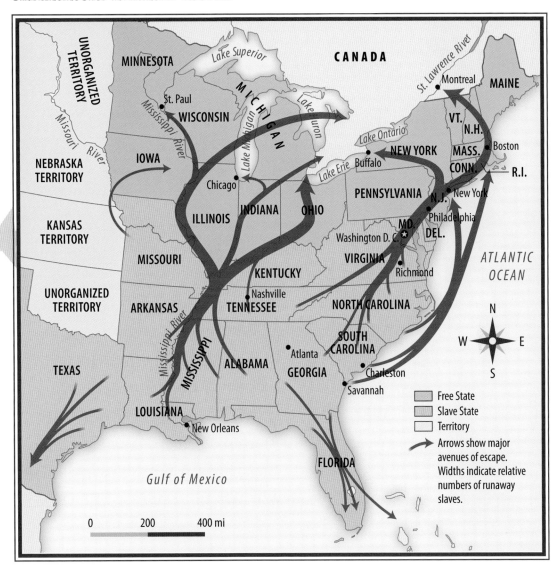

Many escape routes of the Underground Railroad led to the Northern states and to Canada.

CHAPTER 4

NURSE ON THE FRONT LINES

Countless men died in battle during the Civil War. But even more men died from disease and illness. Nurses filled the battlefields. They provided medical help to wounded soldiers. Nurse Clara Barton was so devoted to her work that she earned the nickname "Angel of the Battlefield."

Clara Barton

Barton was a go-getter long before the Civil War began. Born in Massachusetts in 1821, she first worked as a teacher. Later she moved to Washington, D.C. Barton became the first female clerk for the U.S. Patent Office. When the war started in 1861, Barton quit her job. She heard the army was short on supplies and she wanted to help.

Clara Barton, 1886

Barton didn't waste any time. She immediately began tearing up old sheets to use as towels for the soldiers. She also gathered much-needed supplies. Barton traveled to the front lines to deliver the supplies. There she comforted injured men. She also made food and provided water. She put herself in grave danger to help the soldiers. Barton saw some of the war's bloodiest battles. But she never stopped working, even when she was sick with typhoid fever. Her commitment to the troops earned her the title of superintendent of nurses.

After the Civil War ended, Barton continued to help the troops. She led a campaign to find missing soldiers. She published lists of missing men in newspapers. She wrote to soldiers' families.

Throughout her life Barton devoted herself to helping others. She risked her life countless times. But as she once famously said, "You must never so much as think whether you like it or not, whether it is bearable or not; you must never think of anything except the need, and how to meet it."

campaign: an organized effort

Clara Barton's former home is now a museum. Visitors to the museum can learn more about Barton's life.

Barton's Legacy Lives On

In 1869 Barton traveled to Europe for her health. In 1870 she became involved in a war between France and Germany. An organization called the Red Cross was helping French citizens affected by the fighting. Barton offered her help.

Barton returned to the United States in 1873. She soon started the American Red Cross. This group helps victims of wars and natural disasters. Today it carries on Barton's work of helping people in need.

CHAPTER 5

SPIES IN DISGUISE

During the Civil War, men were often suspected of working as spies. But women often went under the radar. Most people didn't think women would want to be spies. For female spies, society's expectations worked to their advantage.

Elizabeth Van Lew and Mary Elizabeth Bowser

Elizabeth Van Lew grew up in the Southern state of Virginia. She came from a wealthy family that owned slaves. Van Lew herself did not agree with slavery. After her father died in 1851, she freed all her family's slaves.

Elizabeth Van Lew

One of these newly freed slaves was Mary Elizabeth Bowser. Van Lew saw how smart Bowser was. She sent her to Philadelphia to attend school. When the Civil War began, however, Bowser returned to Virginia. There, she worked for Van Lew as a spy.

Van Lew helped Bowser get a job working at the Confederate White House. It was a bold and risky move. However, Bowser played her part flawlessly. She pretended to be uneducated so Confederate leaders would speak freely around her. These men had no idea Bowser was giving their secret plans to the Union. Most assumed she was a slave. But they had seriously underestimated her.

Bowser was secretly taking note of every conversation she overheard at the Confederate White House. Her keen memory made her a top-notch spy. She would report back to Van Lew and recite word for word the plans she had heard. Van Lew gave Union leaders the secret information. She made a secret code to send these messages.

Van Lew and Bowser used bravery and brains to outsmart the enemy. If caught they would have been severely punished. They could have been killed. But they were dedicated to their cause. Their efforts likely helped the Union win the war.

MISS VAN LEW'S CIPHER CODE

Van Lew's secret code was written as pairs of numbers. Leaders used this cipher to read the messages.

underestimate: to think something is less important than it really is

Unnamed Heroes of the Civil War

History leaves us with a few accounts of famous Civil War women. But thousands more made heroic efforts day after day. Women whose husbands left home to fight often had to take men's jobs. They entered the workforce and served as clerks and factory workers. They even took charge of family businesses and managed family farms.

For many American women, these jobs were only the beginning. Women also had to care for their homes and families. Just like the brave Civil War women who became famous, these women helped shape the history of the United States.

Men and women worked together in factories making weapons for the Civil War.

A Spy for the Other Side

Rose O'Neal Greenhow was a well-known society woman. She lived in Washington, D.C. She spied on the Union leaders. Then she passed the information to the Confederates. One of her messages may have helped the Confederates win the First Battle of Bull Run.

Greenhow was eventually discovered and put under house arrest. But she continued to pass along messages with the help of other women. She later traveled to Great Britain and France. She spoke out in support of the Confederacy. She met with government leaders. She even published a book called *My Imprisonment and the First Year of Abolition Rule at Washington*.

Greenhow returned to the United States by boat. Tragically, her boat was damaged and she drowned. The Confederates saw her as a hero. Like the Union women, Greenhow risked her life for what she believed in.

The Confederates won the First Battle of Bull Run. The battle was so bloody that both sides knew the war would be long and hard.

Hidden Messages

During the Civil War, spies couldn't text or e-mail messages. They often had to write messages on paper and hide them in their clothing. Women were known to hide messages . . .

in a parasol.

inside their buns or bonnets.

in a purse or hankie.

under their big hoop skirts.

in secret compartments inside the soles of their shoes.

Glossary

abolitionist (ab-uh-LI-shuhn-ist)—a person who worked to end slavery

autobiography (aw-tuh-by-AH-gruh-fee)—a book in which the author tells about his or her life

campaign (kam-PAYN)—an organized effort

front line (FRUHNT LYN)—the area nearest enemy fire

inequality (in-i-KWAH-luh-tee)—lack of the same rights for everyone

plantation (plan-TAY-shuhn)—a large farm found in warm areas; before the Civil War, plantations in the South used slave labor

secede (si-SEED)—to withdraw formally from a group or an organization, often to form another organization

segregation (seg-ruh-GAY-shuhn)—the practice of keeping groups of people apart, especially based on race

suffrage (SUHF-rij)—the right to vote

underestimate (uhn-dur-ES-ti-muht)—to think something is less important than it really is

Read More

Baumann, Susan K. *Harriet Tubman: Conductor of the Underground Railroad.* Jr. Graphic African-American History. New York: PowerKids Press, 2014.

Hamen, Susan E. *Clara Barton: Civil War Hero and American Red Cross Founder.* Military Heroes. Edina, Minn.: ABDO Pub., 2010.

Horn, Geoffrey M. *Sojourner Truth: Speaking Up for Freedom.* Voices for Freedom. New York: Crabtree Pub., 2010.

Critical Thinking Using the Common Core

1. The author wrote, "These women proved that the pen can really be mightier than the sword." Use evidence from the book to show why a reader might agree with this conclusion. (Key Ideas and Details)

2. The author uses fact boxes and sidebars throughout the book. Look on page 26 to find the Mary Elizabeth Bowser fact box. What does the fact box tell you about Bowser? Why did the author include this information in the book? Why wasn't the information included in the main paragraphs? (Craft and Structure)

3. What is the author's opinion about the role of women during the Civil War? Do you agree with her? How did she use evidence to support her point of view? (Integration of Knowledge and Ideas)

Internet Sites

FactHound offers a safe, fun way to find Internet sites related to this book. All of the sites on FactHound have been researched by our staff.

Here's all you do:

Visit *www.facthound.com*

Type in this code: 9781491407196

Super-cool stuff! Check out projects, games, and lots more at **www.capstonekids.com**

Index